# RETURNING TO FIRST NATURE

by Karen Kellock Ph.D.

---

## Manual for Superior Men

A complete theory based on Einstein physics,
Political Psychology, Systems Theory
and Archetypal Psychiatry.

### FORMULA

All success attraction
All disease obstruction
All recovery elimination

You must fast on all three

### OBSTRUCTIONS:

People
Habit
Food

# RETURNING TO FIRST NATURE

## AFTER SCAPEGOAT SYSTEMS

Without gossip and lying they can't spread their hate-filled agenda of ostracizing you forever. Triangulation is about a bitter, hateful and manipulative narcissist trying to control all of us. Victims are relieved knowing it's a major demonic stronghold: the scapegoat. Common treachery: If you're tangled up with a narc and his flying monkey get ready for abuse by proxy. Super Covert: while appearing innocent he stirs the pot then sit backs to watch chaos as a family rots. One ends toxic generational abuse by walking away from other members too. It takes courage to do this or it's a dark cloud in a hell pit.

# GIVE UP ON THE HICKS

IT'S THE CHOSENS WHO STRUGGLE
THEY TRAP YOU TO FAIL
*YOU* CONTROL YOUR FUTURE
NARCS ARE BAGS OF CONTRADICTION
MOVE OUT THE WAY FOR SAFETY
THE WOMAN IS ON EMPTY
SLIPPERY SLOPES FROM DOPES
SHE TURNS ON YOU SUDDENLY
CUT EM OFF TO SAVE YOURSELF
THEY SEE THE CHOSEN AS SNOBS
DESTINY IS ALL ABOUT WAITING
DON'T BRAG ABOUT FASTING, DO IT
THERE'S ALWAYS MORE TO DO
FORGET PROVING A POINT
FORGET ABOUT YOUR VALIDATION!
HICKS DON'T UNDERSTAND DREAMS
THEY COULD BUT WON'T SUPPORT YOU

# GIVE UP ON THE HICKS

## IT'S THE CHOSENS WHO STRUGGLE

It's always chosens that are struggling. But with their comeback all come with hands out, begging.

The cannot handle that you went from rock bottom to the mountaintop. They'd rather see you rot.

If they didn't help while you were struggling, why take em back when you're a success, enjoying?

They wanted your blessings and inheritance. So God hid your value in the shadow of the almighty kids.

You gotta see people for who they really are. They're coming to take everything from a star.

Never go back to people who've already exposed themselves. It's your time to be magic elves.

They will blatantly lie in your face & think they're telling the truth. Their father the devil's like that too.

## THEY TRAP YOU TO FAIL

They were nothing but setup artists setting traps for you to fail. They'll even call the cops to avail.

Often God's rejection is for your protection. They tried to knock you off your perch so now they're gone.

They'll try to set you up now too. Never tell em your good news or they'll get a posse to come for you.

Why do you think God hid your value? He knew people wanted to use, destroy, mock and kill you.

# GIVE UP ON THE HICKS

Don't regret nothing happening for God's giving escape from their devaluing. The saving is your hiding.

One way you know you're going to the next level is when your past is coming at you. It's the devil!

Hide, discern, and be happy nothing's happening. For that's foreshadowing mass attractions coming.

They threw you to the curb but now God's showing you off. It's not so funny now as He elevates you up.

### *YOU* CONTROL YOUR FUTURE

You're in control of your own future now. No one left to gaslight or manipulate you, it's fast forward GO.

Whenever you go to the next level you'll have people plottin. Gotta see em for what they are, rotten.

The past tries to get you in a chokehold but God broke those chains so so why go back? DON'T.

You are **FREE** in the name of Jesus. Unless you back in to the sick systems of the past as evil increases.

Your intuition and evil forebodings are on point! Always listen to it/don't do things God won't anoint.

God's in the exposing business. I know it hurts and brings fear but you'll be protected always.

To a worker, solitude is heaven and interruption is hell. A person in chaos can't come outa his shell.

Everyone has a compass inside them. That's your grand intuition and I'd trust it if I were you man.

Just when you did what they want to shut em up they reversed on you to show you who's on top.

# GIVE UP ON THE HICKS

Nothing you can do ever satisfies a narcissist. Its better to ghost em now, you'd be better off sis.

The narc is a bag of contradictions. Whatever you do or say they'll switch up to put YOU down.

## NARCS ARE BAGS OF CONTRADICTION

They beg or cry for your attention so you give it to them then they ghost you so YOU feel rejection.

Protect yourself by knowing their games then form a mental boundary & return to your own life ok.

The minute you need a narcissist you've had it. It's best to know about em then shut up about it.

I know she's an insecure, nagging bully. She's empty inside but don't feel sorry about the snide.

The minute you put a boundary on her here she comes again, whimpering about rejection. Caution!

You feel sorry for her cuz you're a good person. Then you're snagged again & Satan is the reason.

Whatever move you make you can't stay on top. Satan is behind this so watch ANY involvement.

She ghosted you so you ghost her back then she whimpers about it so you adjust it: fact.

## MOVE OUT THE WAY FOR SAFETY

You move outa the matrix and think you're safe. Then she works hard to get you back on her case.

The confusion of even subtle narcissistic abuse brings exhaustion. This is the folie a deux reaction.

# GIVE UP ON THE HICKS

The narc is sick and empty. When she circles back to your locked gate ignore her call/don't feel sorry.

There's nothing--I mean NOTHING--you can do to stay in the game so stay out & return to health ok.

She complains you don't text her anymore so you do so she won't be sore then she ghosts you more.

## THE WOMAN IS ON EMPTY

The woman is empty and run by Satan see, so he's the one you're escaping for it means treachery.

The basis of narcissism is selfish arrogance. That's the engine running her so return to your diligence.

Of course she whimpers when you put a boundary on her but then she suddenly rises up like a bear.

She acts defeated and sad so you conciliate so she'll be glad then she turns against/calls you a cad.

The situation is so slippery & everchanging as she constantly moves to play victim while lying.

You GIVE to her to make her happy/shut her up then she never says thank you until another blowup.

You wanna feel you have family--you want that so bad--so you can't see they're dangerously mad.

## SLIPPERY SLOPES FROM DOPES

Just as you try to solve it there's another problem. There's no winning in this thorny situation.

You want tranquility & stability but since her father the devil's in complicity this isn't possible see.

# GIVE UP ON THE HICKS

You try to help her with knowledge and she only sees it as one-upping/pushing her off her ledge.

She is woefully & horribly empty but don't feel sorry or get re-entanged in her web of treachery.

To solve her emptiness you invite her to know your friends but she gossips about you to them.

## SHE TURNS ON YOU SUDDENLY

You feel you've done good things for her & it makes you happy then she turns on you suddenly.

She's not your friend and never will be. She says you're it but it's just another shenanigan see.

In the contagion of madness the whole family's infected but for scapegoat, only one is elected.

The chosen never reversed on anybody: THEY changed suddenly so we just moved out the way.

Since we cut em off we got beef with em. They made it look like it's us when we just avoided problems.

## CUT EM OFF TO SAVE YOURSELF

When we cut em off to save ourselves we did way better than them and they took it personally man.

As we move up the ladder everyone starts acting differently around us. It's a spiritual war sis.

We aren't born groupies, but individuals. It's only social hypnotism telling us we're inferior if alone.

We're inferior unless we're surrounded by people: what a dumb thing to teach, it is downright evil.

# GIVE UP ON THE HICKS

The individual is always superior to the group, that's the scoop. The group degrades excellence too.

If anyone switched up it was them, but they blame you for it friend. The bad are a dam contradiction.

## THEY SEE THE CHOSEN AS SNOBS

They think we feel better than anyone else. We don't fit in cuz our calling is higher but lower than angels.

They see you as a snob but you never switched up, just transformed to a higher version of yourself.

Having a higher calling of course you don't fit in. The anointing destroys yolks so you have no friends.

What they call friends is really bondages and strongholds. Sticky, wicked bands that's all.

I didn't reject her, I just moved out of the way but the narcissist takes EVERYTHING personally ok.

The only time they wanna be around you is when they feel entitled to the blessings of God TO you.

The higher you go the less you can trust as your circle shrinks to just one til God brings the rest.

While waiting just keep on fasting and praying. Take a bath, watch movies, play music, anything.

## DESTINY IS ALL ABOUT WAITING

The kingdom of God & destiny is all about waiting. It's frustrating but part of the process of becoming.

You've got plenty to keep you busy so forget this time of not knowing for this is when faith comes in.

# GIVE UP ON THE HICKS

I know how it is, you wake up blocked up. Worry bloats so this is the day to fast [remove yokes].

While waiting you have horrible nightmares. You try to analyze them but remain frustrated/scared.

Nightmares are the old past coming up as the old cycle winds up in preparation for the new--look up!

You still have stuff to do. Have you fasted? This is the last ditch effort to clear the old cycle at last.

## DON'T BRAG ABOUT FASTING, DO IT

I hadn't fasted in 4 years but kept talking about it as if an old pro. That's not it--TODAY you must do it bro'.

Things get so bad it's the fast that is called for now. It's the only way to clear out for the future: wow!

Worry & waiting can cause water retention--bloat--and it's another block needed to clear out now.

What makes it worse is perfidious exits of friends and family but the fast will clear this too, finally.

When those you helped the most are so disloyal it's a helluva thing to digest ya know, so fast now.

Don't do a thing right now, just wait in silence. God will take care of everything but you need a hiatus.

We always think we're done before we are. This is where patience comes in to be that star.

## THERE'S ALWAYS MORE TO DO

There's always more to do before you're revealed. Only God knows that, so just fast and be healed.

# GIVE UP ON THE HICKS

There comes a time in the process that ANY food is poison. It's time to fast, this is your season.

Forget these people. Just continue pressing to the mark of the high calling in Jesus and forget this evil.

When they slam the door in your face God'll remove the ceiling blocking the limitless sky ok? Just wait

You're destined for greatness, doing all things thru Christ. If they don't applaud, have joy despite.

**FORGET PROVING A POINT**

You don't have to prove a point to your family, just make a joyful noise unto the Lord and stay happy.

We are the sheep in His pasture so enter His courts with praise. Family and friends don't mean shit ok.

Be thankful for all He's given you [look around] and bless His holy name for He is good, that's all ok?

When your ship comes in it'll be like a torrent so just wait in peace as nothing's happening friend.

So what if people don't celebrate you, God's getting ready to prove a point THROUGH you Sue!

**FORGET ABOUT YOUR VALIDATION!**

It seems you can't get any celebration, validation or appreciation but your greater is coming hon'.

You don't have to prove a point to those dull family members cuz God saw it all before birth sir.

God saw it before you went into that pit, how your family gave up and gossiped about all of it.

# GIVE UP ON THE HICKS

You shown bright like a diamond & they sold you out anyway. That's all I gotta say of friends & family.

If it had not been for the Lord who was on your side where would you be? Dead, by friends/family.

You can't tell small minded people your big dreams. That's why the chosen are so lonely see.

## HICKS DON'T UNDERSTAND DREAMS

How can you explain your dreams to those who are committed to misunderstanding you bro'?

They have to tools to realize your dreams but they're so busy hating on you it'll never happen see.

As a chosen you don't need your so-called friends to support you. God will bring you everything Sue.

So you gotta wait a few more days, so what? It's been decades suffering blocks. Just fast, pray, look up.

You have a dream, a vision. It's how you know you've made it to top: they can finance you but will not.

In these last evil days you can't speak of your dreams. You're like dreamer Joseph who was hated see.

Joseph's own brothers hated him for his dreams, so wait for it: it will happen to you, you'll soon see.

Even if you were to find someone committed to your dreams, you start arguing about methods see.

My God, all these things! The fast is the last step to break blocks from the treacherous earthlings.

The fast will make these urgent feelings dissolve into "thin" air. You'll see, it's elation I declare!

# GIVE UP ON THE HICKS

The fast is the ultimate humility, making yourself small so God can be BIG and give you the ALL.

Fast, and within a short time everything will fall into place and problems will seem as nothing ok.

Enjoy the moment, for gratitude is the key to God's heart and giving you more. Look around and explore.

## THEY COULD BUT WON'T SUPPORT YOU

They have the money/methods to produce your dreams but they won't. So what? God is on the throne!

You don't need your hometown, family or friends to support you. They aint dreamers! Just schemers.

It's time you let the entire past go: all former things to be blocked out in mind as God said from old.

Be more like Joseph. Sometimes God had to throw you in the pit so you'd wake up/let all people go.

All you have is your SELF. Know this: as long as you have King Jesus you don't need anyone else.

The type of food is important. Try carb cycling: alternate between high and low carb and see.

Fast for one day to clear the slate. Then change your diet totally and then see what happens ok.

You wanna shake things up a bit: see if that changes it. Food is important but a day fast is the catalyst.

You're blocked up from tension. Clean the social slate and the fast to elate then re-start the engine.

You have much to look forward to in today's fast. Getting rid of all the current problems at last.

# SEE THE SNAKES

KEEP YOUR GRASS LOW
ROUTINE BALANCES CHAOS
BEING NICE IS NOT NICE
THEY WANT YOUR ENERGY
YOU GOTTA TRAIN PEOPLE
THEY NEVER RETURN ANYTHING
FIRST THEY TAKE YOUR GLOW
YOU'RE TOO VALUABLE FOR THIS
SATAN SEEKS TO STEAL AND KILL
SATAN SEEKS TO BLOCK SUCCESS
THEY GHOST WHEN YOU'RE CLOSE
POSITIVE WON'T BLOCK EM
SELF-GENTLENESS IS KEY

# SEE THE SNAKES

## KEEP YOUR GRASS LOW

Keep your grass low to reveal snakes. You don't wanna be lovebombed again, pray for discernment ok.

You're too nice, vulnerable and gullible until you never take it again, then discernment is your friend.

There is so much God wants from you and for you but we have an enemy who'd love to derail you.

God allowed me to go thru that with people to finally get my attention and it's the same with you son.

These things had to happen: so I'd mature and grow in the fear and admonition of God, He allowed.

You must be disciplined out here in a cruel world. The chaos around made me that way: strong willed.

## ROUTINE BALANCES CHAOS

Rigid routines balanced outer chaos & laziness and sober focus compensated all the ruckus.

Staying in the will of God allows you to be alert to all the spirits trying to play you--lovebombers too.

As the blessings get closer the attacks get greater, so stay focused on God for He is your Protector.

I said "how come people are always taking advantage of me" and God said "cuz you allowed it, see".

# SEE THE SNAKES

When you see you were too accessible to these people you saw they were NEVER accessible to you!

Even if you warmed to those who did you wrong, the relationship won't be the same for long.

By getting re-entangled you're not available to those who do you right: think about that angle.

Why do we always forgive the toxic people? They get far more chances to come back tho' so evil.

## BEING NICE IS NOT NICE

Being too nice is not nice. You'll for sure only be taken advantage of over and over again, aye.

Don't be available and you're price tag will go way up. I promise you, you'll be valuable not a chump.

Your energy is worth more than silver and gold. It's worth millions man so be certain and bold.

Everyone doesn't deserve to be around you: the way you carry yourself and love, it's rare too.

Every time people see you you're winning, glowing and shining. That's worth millions, no kidding.

The reason you've fallen out with all is cuz God is showing they shouldn't have access at all.

## THEY WANT YOUR ENERGY

It's your energy they want/should be protected. Don't be accessible, that's the behavior to be corrected.

God chose you before the foundation of world. You're NOT for everybody, that's why He did girl.

# SEE THE SNAKES

Why do you chase after this and that when YOU'RE the prize? They should be choosing you, aye.

You have the spirit of the divine on you, destroying the yoke--that's why mass attractions are evoked.

When people get too close ask for a hundred feet. We gotta move too fast for people to impede.

You ain't hard up for lovebombing nor handshake. Make em give you fifty feet--back up and go away!

## YOU GOTTA TRAIN PEOPLE

You gotta train people how to treat you. You're such a breath of fresh air they'd crowd all over you.

But we're sweet, we wanna be accessible instead of standing back and really testing them all.

When you're getting to know people or do business with them take your time. Don't be so dam nice!

When you're with family/friends your guard shouldn't be down. The bible demands vigilance for a reason.

You gotta stay CAUTIOUS. That is the order of the day, this isn't the time to be too nice.

People will turn on you in a blink of an eye. That's the way it is now, there is no loyalty/decency, aye.

People betray with a Judas kiss. They smile in your face but behind your back they can't stand you Miss.

## THEY NEVER RETURN ANYTHING

They never return anything, esp. your energy. All they're doing is draining you, that's their strategy.

# SEE THE SNAKES

They don't see the best in you, only the worst. God sees the best, He's your champion not this curse.

When you love em from a distance & cut em off: that's when you get your power back: lift off!

Cut em off for good and that's then you get your aura back--your beauty, energy and success: fact.

Energy is contagious. If you're accessible to these people you start acting like them: evil.

You start looking dark & pale. You have no light to you: no shine, just stale. You mal-adapt & fail.

You let people use and drain you yet they can't stand you. It's the lowest in the crab bucket Sue.

## FIRST THEY TAKE YOUR GLOW

First they take your glow by throwing shade on your success then you pick up their habits sis.

Don't even be accessible to handshakes or hugs by these predators, especially the latter.

Handshakes & hugs is an energy transfer and it means spirits to deal with later: it's a real bummer.

People carry weird & odd spirits which are energy dead and that explains the stupid ideas in their head.

Realize we're living in the last days when evil spirits are roaming around so don't be accessible ok?

The devil is roaming around like a lion seeking who he can devour so stay watchful every day & hour.

While keeping your grass low ask God constantly to reveal the snakes & never get complacent ok.

# SEE THE SNAKES

I was a dam yes woman and they took everything I had man. Snakes are everywhere, they are demons.

People are stalking you as you come to your winning season. It's more important than ever son.

Continue to put God first in all you do. Then you'll be safe in this latter day warzone so cruel.

## YOU'RE TOO VALUABLE FOR THIS

You're just too valuable in this season to be losing any kind of value. Don't waste one minute Sue.

You must be disciplined when around these energy vampires. You must not let them in, these liars.

Once you see MOST are like this in these latter days, it becomes easier as everyone's suspect ok.

As stressful as it is, if you're ready for them every minute life will go smoothly without surprises/fits.

You can't make any money being emotional. No matter what they did you gotta get calm to grow.

You must train your mind to be in control of emotions, then you'll be unstoppable with gumption.

When you're on your way to the next level--the big bag--the devil likes to play mental tricks like a nag.

## SATAN SEEKS TO STEAL AND KILL

Satan wants to fill your mind with negative thoughts and bad memories. Pretty tricky isn't he.

He reminds you of what evil family members did to you, of ex lovers or friends, the whole ugly stew.

# SEE THE SNAKES

You can be on top of the world and all it takes is that one narcissist to pull you down in a whirl.

## SATAN SEEKS TO BLOCK SUCCESS

Outrageous: Satan doesn't want you to get to that money, to be elated, to be suddenly famous.

When you see ups & downs of life you gotta laugh it off cuz your greater is coming: keep that thought.

As your blessings get closer the attacks become greater. That you must plan on but God's your Protector.

On the way to the next level your past keeps coming back to pull you down/embarrass you to hell.

Every time you get a glimpse of your future the devil gets you in a chokehold and you begin to wonder.

We get emotional over people who are fickle/two-faced. Have we not had enough of the human race?

Remove all your trust in man and put it in God. These are the latter days, you can't trust the flawed.

All it takes is one bad fruit to spoil the whole crate. You can't be careful enough in these latter days.

People don't have the energy you have. They need you but you don't need them, that's the fact.

They are negative & petty, living a toxic life. Without discipline & clarity their bad influence is rife.

## THEY GHOST WHEN YOU'RE CLOSE

When you're that close to breakthru & they have the nerve to ghost you don't let it affect your mood.

# SEE THE SNAKES

You're this close to your miracle and Satan wants to break you. Don't cave in or you won't make it Sue.

Every time you go back to evil friends or your family it's the same problem: low vibrational energy.

You can't change these people, only God can. And they haven't asked Him for that so forget it man.

If you see even **ONE** red flag you must remove yourself. Cuz energy is contagious and you're a magic elf.

## POSITIVE WON'T BLOCK EM

You can be the most positive person but if you hang with the toxic that energy will invade you quick.

Why haven't you made it to the next level? Due to hindering spirits like bad memory from the devil.

You've got so much energy: from love, creativity & optimistic positivity but spirits hinder it see.

Instead of constantly pressing forward you go back to hindering spirits pushing you backwards.

Spiritual warfare is running rampant right now. You can't ever get ahead cuz you won't disallow.

Now press forward to that mark of your highest calling in Jesus. That's all I gotta say sis.

Keep it in your mind that when bad memory comes up it's Satan trying to trigger & block you up.

Those old friends you were so impressed with then are just hindering spirits and bad associations.

Every time you have a bad memory, just as you're about to achieve your destiny, it's Satan see.

# SEE THE SNAKES

You cannot make money if you're always distracted. That's Satan's goal, to keep you nuts with it.

As you approach the goal things build up til you wanna burst. This is when you make gold first.

Hold in the frustration til you blow your lid. That's when the transformation occurs then you'll be lit.

**SELF-GENTLENESS IS KEY**

Time to take a bath or a nap. Be gentle with yourself as you go thru this transmutation of energy gap.

Just as I approached the goal it all went wrong. That's how it works: knowing this keeps you strong.

As the transmutation of energy occurs, everything will come together suddenly & you'll be so happy.

I was hungry, unhoused and going thru hell then everything turned around and all went well.

While on earth the chosen have an adversary & he fights us every inch of the way. Stay in prayer today.

You cannot get there being in your feelings and emotional about what someone did to you.

You've been in alignment with God and thus you're close to the goal with attacks coming constantly, oh!

God hasn't forgotten about you, this wait is part of the process and it can be a depressing time sis.

When you feel like giving up it may be a sign you're very close by just that much. Persevere, buck up.

# RETURNING TO FIRST NATURE

RELEASING BAD RELATIONSHIPS
IT'S UNNATURAL AND YOU KNOW IT
YOU MUST QUARANTINE *NOW*
PERVERSE TRIANGLES ARE STRONGHOLDS
LITTLE MEN PLAYING MR. BIG
ONLY SPIRIT BRINGS DOWN STRONGHOLDS
IT'S YOUR SOCIAL DISTANCING
STOP SWEEPING IT UNDER THE RUG
CHOOSE YOUR PAIN AND DECIDE
SHOT OUT IN LEFT FIELD
FEED OFF SPIRIT/BODY IS SERVANT
BUM OBSESSIONS VS LIFE VISIONS
VISION IS LIKE RETURNING HOME
PUT YOUR FOOT DOWN *NOW*
THE VISION MAKES YOU BUSY DOIN'
LASTLY, MUST ACCEPT ACCOUNTABILITY
ENLIST ONE TRUSTED PERSON
NO MORE BEGGING, PLEADING AND CRYING
GRATITUDE AND PTSD
SIN ATTRACTS LOSERS
GET ANIMAL INSTINCTS BACK
GOD SAID ONE GOOD FRIEND
MODERN WOMEN AND CASUAL SEX
REWARD FOR REPENTANCE: PINK CLOUD
A NEW SEASON
WORK THEN WAIT TO BE DISCOVERED
DASTARDLY WORLD OF ABUSE
SCAPEGOATS ARE EMPATHS
SCAPEGOATS DERAILED FROM DESTINY
ALWAYS ABUSE BY PROXY
HOME OF SPITE
DOMINO EFFECT WITHOUT LET UP
NEVER EXPLAIN YOURSELF AGAIN
IT'S ALL BEEN TRIANGULATION
THEY WORE YOU OUT
SEARED CONSCIENCE MELTS DOWN
GREATEST SAINTS WERE THE WORST SINNERS

# RETURNING TO FIRST NATURE

MY GHOST TOWN EXPERIENCE
SEPARATION UNTO STARS AND SAND
TRAUMA BONDS SCREAM FOR CORRECTION
LURKING FOR OLD FLAMES:  STOP IT
INDIVIDUATION FROM THE FAMILY SYSTEM
INSTINCTUAL KNOWLEDGE OF SYSTEMS
THEY'RE LIKE POOH ON THE SHOE
WORK ALL THE TIME/SELF-DETERMINED
MOST OF THE WORLD IS REALLY CREEPY
PUT PAST IN A BAG, THROW IT OUT
GENIUS KNOWS THE VALUE OF LEISURE
JESUS SAID:  NO ONE'S GOOD!
WITHOUT GOSPEL IT'S ALL BABBLE
SINS ERASED FROM EAST TO WEST
SIN TO ESCAPE FATE BRINGS HATE
BACK FROM THE BRINK, A PERFECT SAINT
EARLY GENIUS DEGRADES THE SAME
DESTINY DERAILED BY SENSUAL APPETITES
DIVINE MIRACLES FROM LIVING RIGHT
LOQUACITY:  PEOPLE TALK TOO MUCH
HIGH WALLS, LOCKED GATE:  GOOD FATE
REPENT FOR SELF-LOVE OR ELSE
FRIENDSHIPS ARE TESTED AND TRIED!
GOD USES ENEMIES TO DISCIPLINE YOU!
FINDING THE QUINTESSENTIAL-ONLY
IT WASN'T THEM, *SIN* BRINGS ATTACKS
ARROGANCE PRECEDES RUIN
MIXED SIGNALS OF THE RABBLE
DON'T SUCCUMB: RISE ABOVE PTSD
FORGIVE BUT NOT FORGET
SELF-CHOSEN FAMILIES
SOCIAL IS *NOT* SUPERIOR
COMMUNISM TRIGGERED BY RACISM
HISTORICAL REVISIONISM
HIX PEEVED OVER POLITIX
THE MORE LOFTY THE HIGHER THE WALLS
MAGIC OF STARVATION

# RETURNING TO
# FIRST NATURE
## *Preface*

### RELEASING BAD RELATIONSHIPS

**RESET: Create in me a clean heart Lord and renew a right spirit within me. It's beyond us see.**

**We can create bondage and strongholds for ourselves but it's impossible to get out without God.**

**It's not natural for you to LONG for someone who abuses you. You're smarter than that Sue.**

**You thought you were just having sex. You didn't know you'd be opening spiritual doors to a hex.**

**You have two dissimilar animals yoked together and it's a broken neck or lost dreams forever.**

**The only way out is spiritual. Invite the holy spirit in to uproot the implants and attraction to nuts.**

**There are some things that can't be counseled out. You must invite the holy spirit in to take it out.**

**Stop saying "I hate you" to past introjects long dead but hooked to your sorry soul nevertheless.**

### IT'S UNNATURAL AND YOU KNOW IT

**This thing you're dealing with isn't natural and you know it. You need the holy spirit POWER to rid it.**

**You will love yourself squeaky clean and sweet again, like a little baby innocent and with friends.**

# RETURNING TO FIRST NATURE

Don't sink in the muck and mire with that liar leading you down to hell due to his filthy desires.

You will love your sweet innocent self & abhor that dirty man leading you away from God--block him.

Is it natural to be addicted to one having nothing to offer--stallion and donkey yoked together?

**YOU MUST QUARANTINE *NOW***

Now while the holy spirit's doing his work you must quarantine or go no-contact, that's a fact.

You cannot go into the infected area obviously, that means don't call or see me while healing.

If you keep reinfecting yourself and see him you won't get better. You must allow the spirit resetter.

Every time you search him on social media you reinfect yourself. See this and you're nearly out.

Let gratitude for what He's done cure you of PTSD memory as it disperses then is through.

Instead of ruminating constantly about those little creeps who invaded me I thank God see.

When we move away from God we create our own bondage but if in Him there's clearance.

We discern origination of the tie--deferred hope, perversion, trauma, insecurity--then it dies.

**PERVERSE TRIANGLES ARE STRONGHOLDS**

Things like perverse triangles cause strongholds but ask God to remove them and out they go.

# RETURNING TO FIRST NATURE

It should be very comforting knowing God gave us a simple way out of this painful problem.

Create in me a clean heart and take out everything acting as a magnet to maggots see.

What made you fall in love with a creepy little man so different from your dad? You went bad.

Enantiodromia means everything converts to it's opposite--a sweet kid became a monster.

Sudden reversals in personality indicate a stronghold or soul tie--spiritual knots in the system, aye.

**LITTLE MEN PLAYING MR. BIG**

What made you allow a little man playing Mr. Big to take over your life? A block cuz you left God.

Take it out dear Lord, take it out. That thing in me that lodged in my soul settling for faithless love.

What is that thing in you making you feel worthless, settling for less and putting up with this?

You're supposed to be a queen taking dominion but due to a knot in the system you love a bum.

The bum steers your whole life and you see him as a god then all your friends think you're odd.

He introduces perversion going against wisdom and that locks you in--a stronghold cuz you weakened.

Once you accept a level of perversion he pushes for more and soon you're in a dark spiritual war.

After years of toiling to break the tie you find the simple answer of God's spiritual weaponry so fine.

# RETURNING TO FIRST NATURE

Lord give me a bath. Uproot every little thing that is unrighteous & shower me with your goodness.

We do not war in flesh for our weapons are not carnal but thru mighty God pull down strongholds.

Our heavily sexualized world is built on soul ties and strongholds, a cobweb of pain and woes.

You never knew you had these mighty spiritual weapons I'll bet: access to the Father's presence.

## ONLY SPIRIT BRINGS DOWN STRONGHOLDS

God said these weapons pull down strongholds--you're problem is denying it/sinking in hell holes.

Soul ties, strongholds, painful split ups, serial adulteries and debaucheries: just ask mighty God see.

If a man pressures you to move in a direction you know is wrong get rid of him now or spiral down.

Stop dismissing yourself as old fashioned. You are God's man and that's eternal not time-bound.

You accept one level of depravity or perversion and you'll go another. Nip it in the bud sister.

In presence of God anything not of Him is made subject. You see that guy carnally but he's demonic.

You have a soul tie with one you've never met. You see him on the net, another disappointment.

You must realize there may be pain and you gotta be strong NOT to search him virtually again.

You must quarantine. Say it again--you MUST or start the painful healing process all over again.

# RETURNING TO FIRST NATURE

Quarantine: this is where personal initiative comes in: sanctification now that you refuse to see him.

Quarantine = sanctification. Separate yourself while God cleans you up to be precious to Him.

Sanctification means to set yourself apart. This is holy--tho' they call you antisocial just ignore it.

## IT'S YOUR SOCIAL DISTANCING

Do your own social distancing. Become rare to the darkly menacing and start a new life singing.

If you're serious about getting better and healthy you gotta quarantine--don't go there/don't see.

No wonder the mental health crisis of teen depression, anxiety and suicide, they're sexualized.

Have you made the decision to separate yourself from this person making your life a prison?

The holy spirit won't make that decision, it just shows the origination and pulls out the problem.

God pulled everything out of me attracted to bad boys in adult bodies. He readied me for kings.

YOU must decide, you must quarantine and separate. Show God you can, refuse to participate.

Decide you want holy wholeness then see the only way is sanctification via separateness.

## STOP SWEEPING IT UNDER THE RUG

Don't sweep things under the rug anymore. There's an undertow with this guy and he's abhorrent.

# RETURNING TO FIRST NATURE

"Come out from among them" God said--it's an instruction for you not Him, you make the decision.

Come out from amongst them, be ye separate and touch not the unclean thing: dump him.

God says if you want my power, the liberty and joy I bring you've gotta leave that alone see.

You've gotta come outa that and I'll receive you but no holding onto Me while continuing pursuit.

It's gotta be either God or "that"--you must choose. Decide, block that old fool, wait to heal.

## CHOOSE YOUR PAIN AND DECIDE

You gotta choose your pain and decide. As long as you're vacillating you're stuck on this ride.

I've experienced love addiction and I know the pain. Of being discarded or jilted, left sad in the rain.

Go thru this short pain and in walks a decent nice man as your life shows gains and happy days.

Either waste your life on a dude God never gave you or cut ties, hurt for a while but heal very soon.

Choose your pain: of longing when he never gave you a thing or temporary pain of quarantine.

He rescued you from outrageous circumstances He found you with, now don't go back to the pit.

Don't recall memories of the pit either--of debaucheries or whatever--for He saved you and it's over.

Don't wake up at the end realizing you wasted your life on something you deserved better than.

# RETURNING TO FIRST NATURE

Pondering [on level/origination], uprooting and quarantine is followed by soul re-centering.

Whenever you think of "him" or "it" just substitute thoughts of God making you pure and legit.

Recap: your new life can't happen until the old one is totally abandoned--it's all up to you hon'

You can't bring balance to soul until living in a bubble for now forming a wall against the old/cold.

Since soul ties are always the produce of spiritual imbalance you must center in silence.

## SHOT OUT IN LEFT FIELD

You got way out in left field with a he who never gave you a thing see, a self-destructive spree.

You thought of nothing but him for months or years, that's a soul tie and a stronghold dear.

You're so much smarter than him but that doesn't matter hon' cuz a soul tie blurs vision.

Soul ties are always from an imbalance between spirit/soul/body and he's the result honey.

They know not what they say but they say it all the time and with great urgency and authority.

You have the strength to rise above and not believe a thing he says just God who purifies the past.

Out of balance: bend to flesh. Wrong order is body first then soul, spirit: all you think about is sex.

Some lead with their soul first, goaded by a worldly intellect and this is doubly problematic.

# RETURNING TO FIRST NATURE

The divine order of God is spirit, soul, body. Just attending church doesn't mean this see.

When I'm spirit-soul-body I'm truly directed by God and all the weaknesses in me are shown out.

The spirit is sensitive to God, the soul takes its orders and then the carnally driven body follows.

## FEED OFF SPIRIT/BODY IS SERVANT

You should feed off the spirit while the body becomes the servant of the soul and that is all.

Now that there's no contradiction between my members people trust me but body-driven was scary.

This I say: walk in the spirit and thee shall not fulfill the lusts of the flesh. Just keep it first it says.

Flesh & world is constantly pulling you. Center in spirit cuz that's half the battle in the human zoo.

Be not conformed to this world but transformed by the renewing of your MIND. What a relief, aye.

She's so preoccupied with a little bum he's all she thinks about and she's forgotten her Life Vision.

My my my. You're reading this while consumed by a bum and worse: forgetting your purpose hon'

## BUM OBSESSIONS VS LIFE VISIONS

You've forgotten your purpose/why the Creator made you and not even using your rare gifts too.

While trapped in a soul tie all you think about is sex--it's swept you up into a net of wasted gifts.

# RETURNING TO FIRST NATURE

You're so broken you've stopped reaching for destiny cuz God kicked the bum out finally?

A broken woman says "you get over one man by getting under another" as she's again plundered.

You need to return to yourself not get under another man or follow any silly dangerous slogan.

Girl, you don't need another man til you got your mind right and your soul centered: new plan.

Get pen/pad and write down why you're here and stop talking to us about this little bum sister.

When God kicks a bum from your life when you couldn't thank him not cry for months still smitten.

He's lettered, comes from a good family and has money but he's still a BUM if you see him clearly.

## VISION IS LIKE RETURNING HOME

As God rescued me from the maelstrom I returned to my vision and felt so happy to be home again.

The reward for returning to your vision is God will remind you how valuable you are then and again.

You always lose yourself when running behind someone else but now you've returned as a magic elf.

And thus soul ties divorce you from yourself and your future and to me this was horrible torture.

I'm only happy writing cuz God told me to, not fighting with a bum due to a spiritual war of cookoo.

And thus where there is no vision the people perish--into the arms of a bum or addictive anguish.

# RETURNING TO FIRST NATURE

It means if you lack a vision of a preferred future you will have no limits, lines, boundaries for sure.

Without a guiding vision your life goes full steam off to the right, the left or fall behind off a cliff.

Without vision you lack boundaries around you nor defenses blocking those time wasters too.

Returning to your vision brings back your limits so line-crossers you instantly know and reject.

You say NO: You deserve better than that and this is totally unacceptable, get rid of that rat.

**PUT YOUR FOOT DOWN *NOW***

You put your foot down now, not a weaselly acceptance of what you don't want from fear of a fall.

Get back to vision, center your soul and never lead with your flesh: NOW you choose what's best.

Returning to vision is becoming enlightened & hardened: she's a no/he's a no and be determined.

You've spent your time sexually obsessed with a clown in a crown never asking why you're around.

Instead of pleading and crying over a bum pay attention to your WHY and it's all replaced with fun.

When you die your legacy is not gonna be who you slept with but how you fulfilled a destiny on earth.

**THE VISION MAKES YOU BUSY DOIN'**

Getting back to your vision you'll be so busy doin' you won't have time to be cryin' over a bum like him.

# RETURNING TO FIRST NATURE

I don't wanna sound like your mother but you've no time to waste cuz you're not getting any younger.

Anguish cuz little bum won't return your calls. Imagine how silly this is from a soul tie that's all.

God says your vision has an Appointed Time. You don't have time to waste, only to prepare, aye!

Get back to vision and it heals your heart from the pain of brokenness--a sycophant to lowness.

## LASTLY, MUST ACCEPT ACCOUNTABILITY

Lastly, you must accept accountability. You were a bit dirty and needed to hear all this honey.

I'm not gonna coddle your dysfunction but shake it up to trash the bloody historical foundation.

You need someone to come in like King Kong and bash the foolishness you've been carrying on.

You must at all costs avoid the pain at end of life realizing you wasted it on a bum and his lies.

While you heal over a hobo let the spirit heal the pain and each day you'll be better you know.

You need me or somebody to tell you to HOLD to the truth and don't waiver one more time too.

Stop running from parents and friends telling you the truth while drowning in an emotional stew.

All of us must have accountability--it's hard to see the picture when you're in the frame honey.

## ENLIST ONE TRUSTED PERSON

# RETURNING TO FIRST NATURE

Give all your details and tendencies to one trusted person who can ascertain the situation.

Tell him how after a few days you go back and beg--they need to know all of it to know your case.

Tell this accountability partner how you stalked him online at 5:00 then again at 7:00, aye.

We then who are strong need to bear the infirmities of the weak. Seek one stronger, then lead.

When you are breaking the grips of a soul tie you need accountability--find that one guide quickly.

**NO MORE BEGGING, PLEADING AND CRYING**

This is the last of your begging, pleading and crying. It's lowered your status in the eyes of many.

Never again will you stalk someone who doesn't even deserve a conversation, it's over hon'.

As you read this and as you pray you're gonna be completely free in Jesus' name: hurray!

Your head will be cleared and your soul centered. Now you're on track to be the healthiest winner.

Your relationships will move forward with greater wisdom, losing your negative perspective.

Now you'll have great discernment and will never again--ever--go thru this spiritual enslavement.

The devil is a liar if he thinks you'll ever lose your life to a bum in a crown or anyone else around.

The bottom feeder thing is done in your life see. God will now keep you high & happy doing His thing.

# RETURNING TO FIRST NATURE

Center your soul, get back to your vision and **FREEDOM** is your portion, in Jesus mighty name amen.

Get outa this soul tie relationship [implant, introject] and you'll be flying sky high as The Elect.

A soul tie is an encumbrance that'll drag you down into hopelessness and its from sex.

Ridding soul ties and strongholds is the last of your studies, then just fly away to creativity.

**GRATITUDE AND PTSD**

I shudder thinking of close calls God saved me from but even that's a spit in His eye son.

Let gratitude for what He's done cure you cure you of PTSD memory and soon it's all through.

Here you're sitting in your castle on east street after he rescued thee and you're still angry see.

Don't dwell on close calls just on the Rescuer of us all and keep your mind focused/no recalls.

So you made a mistake--get offa that thing for a warrior's not encumbered with futile memory.

They fantasize about doing it but when the time comes don't want to, flaking out without a word.

Is this not the second time he's/she's flaked out without a word? it's ghosting and it's rude.

He's not gonna leave his wife, children, reputation and finances to be with you--his side chick.

How to move on: Pay attention to the thoughts you've ignored and swept under the rug hon'

# RETURNING TO FIRST NATURE

**No more the maladapted poser,
I wrote this to not go mad sir.**

When an exalted and energetic female has an introjected demon mother she's a terror.

If the problem's always been other people you'll explode with potential when you're finally alone.

Everyone has skeletons in their closet. Remember that before you go blabbing/confessing all of it.

So you did this or that. Who cares? We all gotta deal with the devil in our affairs until we mature.

Stop worrying about past repeating itself cuz life is a ladder and you'd never again be that engulfed.

Having been thru trauma your boundaries collapsed and maybe even your morals: forget about it.

God removes hedge of protection and the evil world swoops in: holes in your bucket now friend.

You think you're protected with guns and fences but evil always snags you even by taking offense.

**SIN ATTRACTS LOSERS**

The minute I took that first drink evil knocked at my door. It was uncanny, a sign from the Lord.

# RETURNING TO FIRST NATURE

You'd never be so naive to let three creepy young thugs in. No, you'd never be that gullible again.

You're sense of self-protection is innate now, it's in your DNA. You've been trained by sadists ok?

I feel so much pity for my prior self not knowing enough to barricade off from the rabble's guff.

They all wanted a piece of me. I could sense them lurching like a wide gulf/bottomless pit see.

A young naive girl lets wicked men into her home. A lady wouldn't do this ever, esp. if alone.

What do you mean it's different? God'll come against a male slut just as much as a female sir.

It's so scary that the youth are mainly now illiterate and about geography or math don't give a shit.

## GET ANIMAL INSTINCTS BACK

Get primitive impulses back. If someone's bigger than you/you don't know them, block the hick.

You don't know, it could be like putting a rattlesnake in your cage. Get hep like any animal, ok?

I was so poorly defended I even let em in knowing they're scorpions--being a good hostess like mom.

Don't be disabled/consumed with PTSD from lower rungs/decades of dung when a girl so young.

Simply see it all as your Ph.D. in the Streets, a painful boot camp ala separation from creeps.

They were pre-convict teens who looked good even innocent but what a horrible predicament.

# RETURNING TO FIRST NATURE

So your parents never prepared you for the onslaught of sordid expectations of slobs for your bod.

So you were like a fish swimming upstream, choking and screaming with seemingly no one listening.

How'd you know those expectations were creepy and sinful, things they had no right asking for?

Like a dam lemming you went along cuz so did the throng, never questioning a sin kingdom.

The minute she splashed into town the dregs pulled her further down and decades were blown.

Oh bullshit, learn how to think bitch. That's what men think but don't say, never scratching the itch.

So they ignore you with age. See this as FREEDOM cuz now you can finally live your own life ok.

## GOD SAID ONE GOOD FRIEND

God said you'd have ONE friend along the way. Rely on that: like neighbors it's better than family.

They ignored you this long--your whole entire life--so they don't get in now that you're rich, aye?

Mom was snooty--I shoulda listened to that. It was my only preparation as a buffer against brats.

Friends, we're not prepared. Not only can we not trust each other now its unvetted/unknown cultures.

I had no idea what the kids were like, and these were high school '85. Imagine things now, aye.

I thank God every day I'm behind a fence and a locked gate for now every moment is good fate.

# RETURNING TO FIRST NATURE

Happy wives thank God every day they have a husband to protect them from the outside bedlam.

It's absolutely cruel what happens to single women if unique and trying to socially fit in, yikes.

The gender war is won in sexual arena as females dumbly succumb to what men want: idiots!

The sexual is the only place left where men can dominate by emotionally rejecting you mate.

And so the modern woman says she doesn't care either, we can be as dam apathetic as men sister.

This is the drought the bible speaks of. It is mental, theological, emotional, logical: unheard of.

Solution to outer drought: Come within, put fences up, create your own reality and now be happy.

Home is All: Let that be your new slogan. Create your own inner island in a sea of sharks friend.

## MODERN WOMEN AND CASUAL SEX

Modern professional women are suffering invisibly from casual sex wearing them down emotionless.

Trying to be like men all the while giving men what they want: casual sex and one night stands.

Thinking you're superior cuz you do what any cow, goat, dog, cat or lower animals do: have sex.

A mental and spiritual drought is a meaningless existence. Without meaning life is senseless.

With a meaningful life every corner lights up but in a spiritual drought it's just boring humdrum.

# RETURNING TO FIRST NATURE

Giving into all your baser instincts is not freedom--no matter how much the rich think it is son.

He can afford to give in all he wants but the more he does the worst his consciousness gets.

It's called a poverty of ideation man. When your world goes black and all seems hopeless/bland.

That poverty of ideation is from sin and also the sin of bad associations which go together friend.

## REWARD FOR REPENTANCE: PINK CLOUD

The reward of repentance is right-brain living: synchronicity, living in miracle-city, spiffy.

Now I'm back on that pink cloud I'm never going back down in that hellish trap of man w/o God.

He always came around on the day her money came and she never saw the connection ok?

When women view imminent change they set things up ahead of time searching for new kings.

It's just survival and I'm sorry if it seems utilitarian or lowly evolved to plan your life as allowed.

Life is rough in the latter days. It's pure jungle survival of the fittest: think of the widows, girls, boys.

If you're reading this my answer's YES: all you surmise is true and I appreciate your patience too.

We don't just wait for the imminent end, we're the weaker sex and we must plan ahead ma'am.

Don't let gloom take over again. You gotta know God wants you high and happy for your salvation.

# RETURNING TO FIRST NATURE

**A NEW SEASON**

A new season, a new day: power and prosperity, all pains to allay. It's called "blessed"--enjoy God's buffet.

I'm in the groove man, the predestined thing planned before my birth: I'm in the flow, synchronicity now.

Just do your work then wait to be discovered. Only God knows the day or hour but you'll get the power.

Your troubles gave you soul--making you warm, empathic and glowing while the others remained cold.

Fill it with each other = becomes an echo chamber. Fill it with God =continuous revelations so clever.

**DID I WRITE THIS TO NOT GO MAD?**

Did I write it to not go mad or go mad to understand the nature of madness? Holocaust survivor

He's offended I want all night, morning, afternoon for office hours without interruption, hmmm.

Not only is it totally safe here--out of the way, I have never seen such beauty/sweet silence ok.

Creative Act: I just want completion, no more endless spring, to retire and then be a child again.

It's exhausting to be an endless spring, sometimes you're writing for days/nights on end see.

I eat once a day so all energy goes into this. When it comes to a life's work there is nothing else.

68,000 proverbs in twelve years and still it goes on. The Creative Act is a cycle with an end?

# RETURNING TO FIRST NATURE

I want to be a carefree child again with an endless cash flow--that's retirement, pure enjoyment.

Beans, cheese, tomato and corn. What could be more California ala Mexico or delicious you know.

You reach a point where you don't know what day it is or what the hell you're doing here: persevere.

## WORK THEN WAIT TO BE DISCOVERED

You worked and waited, now it happens overnight. In the twinkling of an eye, success out of sight.

It's the price you pay to be a star. People can raise you up but will also pull you down, so beware.

Turn off all shows--it's most important to get into your own thing now.

Those favored by God are hated by man. They hate your success so don't try to explain, just ban.

Having someone tyrannize over you is the best education to be a good leader.

Reason to be sweet, gentle, loving and self-controlled: it saves energy.

Be a pliable paintbrush in the Master's hands. Whether a writer, singer or protestor in the stands.

Your trials give you something to say. Now they'll really hate as God turns your ashes into a bouquet.

It's your time so resume dreaming. Keep that dream alive: no need for scheming, God is redeeming.

You don't need a gift to preach or sing. What gives you power is affliction--then a giant upswing.

We sin to avoid anxiety but then anxiety gets worse, triggering us to sin again--that's how it works.

# RETURNING TO FIRST NATURE

Our God is so good--He gives reprieves till the very end. No matter how sick or failed we can still win.

**DASTARDLY WORLD OF ABUSE**

Flying monkeys are followers only. They don't check the facts like a doctor or professional attorney.

And this is why both the narcissist and his army as so dangerous, the Nazis began like this.

She sent them out guilt-free to hurt me and then sat back innocently while my world crashed see.

Only cowards and women have others do their dirty work and it always turns out meaner of course.

The role of flying monkeys was invisible to me for years, I just didn't like them ever coming over.

It always felt like an invasion, which it was since she primed em to hate me with cruel derision.

She used them as her sidekicks and even the sheriff was one as she'd use him as a bludgeon.

And this is why flying monkeys bow down to emotional vampires like the malignant narcissist.

No matter what you do flying monkeys won't wake up, they can only follow/keep the status quo.

It may help you to know flying monkeys would follow anything handed to them by the narcissist.

It's all BS, a web of lies, there are no facts involving it, it's family mythology calling you the twit.

We have to look at the root of this in all its demonic forms--these guys may be bound forever.

# RETURNING TO FIRST NATURE

## SCAPEGOATS ARE EMPATHS

If you're victim it should bring great relief knowing it's a major demonic stronghold: the scapegoat.

Triangulation is the number ONE tool of every narcissist and that's why she never comes alone sis.

They train monkeys in the art of gossip, lying and planting evil seeds--very shrewd this teaching.

Without gossip and lying they can't spread their hate-filled agenda of ostracizing you forever.

It's not that I was crazy but that I didn't know my limitations then--gotta go solo to be best.

Triangulation is about a bitter, hateful and manipulative narcissist trying to control all of us.

The opinion leader of the tribe does a lot of gaslighting and destroying of relationships like Jeffs.

She will destroy your relationship with husband, children, grandchildren, coworkers, all of em.

## SCAPEGOATS DERAILED FROM DESTINY

We return to our first nature thru the erasure of all social hypnotic adaptations and attractions.

We scapegoats are paving the way for freedom from toxic abusive siblings and full recovery.

Half truths or once-in-a-time blunders tangled up in a web of lies as if it's all of her life forever.

Blatant lies about me which were so ugly and gross man cuz they have dirty minds those harridans.

# RETURNING TO FIRST NATURE

Triangulating & brainwashing, gaslighting & gossiping then stalked & hounded by flying monkeys.

There's a root of evil sinister motives cuz anyone with a sound mind would never do any of this.

Sound minds wouldn't destroy your relationships. Sound minds create happy environments.

People who love you will not turn their back on you, deny the truth or go in with the shrews.

We evolve thru the years. Start in a dark cocoon feeling trapped with no way out then free: mature.

You'll never relapse into sheepish doormat status, life is a metamorphosis and now you're top most.

Sibling abuse is rampant cuz liberalism is. Conservatives are rare, souls stuck in sick systems.

Tell us about your experience with triangulation, ruined relationships and smear campaigns.

A man who won't leave me in another city? I cling to him like rubies, from bad to good guys.

After I proved to God I appreciated living in a ghost town He gave me mansions to enjoy now.

First of all, you need no one but yourself. Passionate attractions are soul ties and false.

Feeling like you can't live without him, gotta have him, wanna merge--indicates soul ties, a curse.

Anxious people foresee disaster. Hardly anyone sleeps peacefully. This is how we lived constantly.

**ALWAYS ABUSE BY PROXY**

# RETURNING TO FIRST NATURE

Common treachery: If you're tangled up with a narc and flying monkey get ready for abuse by proxy.

They want you to overreact--cry and scream--so the monkey returns to the narcissist esteemed.

The narcissist craves this dysfunction, denial and deception. He loves chaos and bedlam.

Super Covert: Narc uses flying monkeys to abuse the scapegoat while appearing innocent.

The narc will stir the pot, stir the pot then just sit back and watch the chaos as the family rots.

You can be getting along so nicely then all hell breaks loose after they triangulated them too.

People talk, and they talk. All our problems stem from triangulation since people aren't an island.

One decides to end toxic generational abuse--by walking away from every single member too.

It takes phenomenal courage and bravery to do this but the alternative is a dark cloud in a hell pit.

## HOME OF SPITE

He snatched me from a dark cobweb and put me in a safe place and new house with nice friends.

The minute I got married she stopped sniping at me. She even apologized--they see only categories.

Why be around niece or nephew when confirming the narc is all they do, coming against you too?

Home was a dark cavern of spite and people who despised me but I had a vision of destiny.

# RETURNING TO FIRST NATURE

My relation to them was how the devil was coming thru to me. I felt stressed and sad constantly.

Desperately in need of protection I married a loser whose three kids drove me down further.

We make wrong decisions then more wrong decisions 'til decades have gone by in confusion.

To see it as abuse then to say Enough is Enough I'm not gonna play your game anymore chumps.

## DOMINO EFFECT WITHOUT LET UP

He had no lines really and his three kids were hillbillies in how they sought supply and treated me.

There are members who forever justify the narc and blame-shift to the embattled scapegoat.

When we're free of the narc, his monkeys and the crazy making dynamics we're free of BONDAGE.

As long as it's you--strong empath--against a tribe of weaklings you're unequally yoked, weeping.

Why talk with those against you/getting others against you and who retaliate with smear campaigns?

When we walk away from trauma bonds, triangulation and relationship-destruction new life begins.

After walking away waste no more time explaining yourself. What a relief, you've said it all.

## NEVER EXPLAIN YOURSELF AGAIN

Remember, you're thru explaining yourself. Tell US--the world--about it for its really quite obvious.

# RETURNING TO FIRST NATURE

People are malicious--filthy rags--and who do they have to abuse but their sibling? Wake up/it's bad.

We are paving the way for them to restore after trauma, to make sense out of a senseless mama.

The whole healthy boundary and recovery program is based on blessing and releasing them.

Bless and release, bless and release: like a chick pecking outa the eggshell, adios to hell.

Why total walkaway: your relationships triangulated to such a degree every one is tainted see.

## IT'S ALL BEEN TRIANGULATION

It's best to relocate, since they've triangulated the postman, the sheriff and neighbors too ok.

Why did people fall for evil gossip? We can't say always except weakness sides with lunatics.

Why does anyone buy evil gossip? For the same reason the same person falls for any nonsense.

After recovery we seek whole relationships: MUTUAL, loving, caring, vulnerable, soul-bearing.

At the end of the day, life is too short to tolerate destructive relationships, no how/no way.

No, never defend yourself to those who triangulated ALL of your relationships for decades.

## THEY WORE YOU OUT

They wore you out: constant war by magicians behind scenes but then God restores your youth see.

# RETURNING TO FIRST NATURE

The gnawing sense of sad hopelessness never left until I did like the courageous who manned up.

Them still justifying those who died is same as with you the victim of the malicious and snide.

Think of the rest, in a pit and can't find their way out. And then one day liberty, they're empowered.

Born clear we arrive in a system awaiting us. We adapt to an evil matrix til your words saved us.

They wore me out/I aged overnight. My bones creaked, my skin just hung then God made me a knight.

Now whole and confident you connect with likeminded people who respect you, who "get" you.

These new friends will love you despite your flaws since we're not perfect and you will know it.

## SEARED CONSCIENCE MELTS DOWN

A point is reached when seared conscience melts down. A period of tears follows then the Self is found.

In elder years the temporal lobes open up to reveal eternity: panoramic perception in a smaller body.

Born clear we mal-adapt to an insane world and the smartest get the sickest or they find the pearl.

It is the fact I could never please them that I got so good cuz it compelled constant improvement.

If insecurity compels constant improvement then maybe that's God's plan but eventually let it go, man.

It's not that you created a higher reality, it's that you repented and God gave it to you mightily.

# RETURNING TO FIRST NATURE

To make a dent in society we must be famous--that's obvious--but can we handle it? Must do it.

After much suffering I asked God for help and He brought me back with a Creative Act--done, in fact.

Dark night of the soul: Daily tears, God's curse: used to educate us and prepare for battle of course.

In the fallen hero syndrome, boundaries dissolve and evil worlds flow in to the end of you/your home.

Dark night of the soul is over. What a curse but I learned so much and now it's time for takeover.

## GREATEST SAINTS WERE THE WORST SINNERS

Since the greatest saints were the worst sinners the best future can spring from the worst past.

What made Jesus' speech powerful was word pictures and that's also true of Einstein/all discoverers.

I just want someone who's neat and nice--is there anyone left like that or is it way too much to ask?

They must adapt to you or you'll never get anything done. You're problem is being eclipsed by them!

How could I know my foes were my friends--it was always them that was "loving and good" they said.

Let em go, people aren't important. It's God, He's first and foremost--men move, die or go dormant.

It's hard to get her out of her home even if she's moving up higher because it's what she's known.

I know we get busy but don't forget to party cuz the incapacity for leisure blocks genius or the arty.

# RETURNING TO FIRST NATURE

Can't rush ahead and force it myself. I've learned that from false starts, humiliating failures/God Himself.

I've done my work, it's complete. But am I going to market myself? Never, all problems He'll meet.

Be an exemplar in your generation. That's opposite to them--it takes strength not to slide down.

Yes he's the king of narcissism/egotism but we love it cuz God designed self it's like a magic elf.

If your motives are good you can be as arrogant/conceited as you please, just not a cheat/sleaze.

## MY GHOST TOWN EXPERIENCE

The desert wilderness was vast space--nothingness. I had to expand my inner realms just to make sense.

Defined by the cultural narrative and the details of my own situation, suddenly these were long gone.

No one gave a dam that I had a Ph.D. in psychology! All the more reason to think I was crazy.

No car, no TV/internet, no friends. Just dogs and my two legs and we walked all over the 1000 acres.

I always loved beauty and design in architecture yet here I adored a dusty shack built 100 years before.

My mind was transported to another era and it fascinated me. A mental transport as it were, I felt free.

Social acculturation is mimicking each other, she marched to another drummer and they abhorred her.

In nothingness I found God. He was blotted out with all my distractions but He was all I thought of now.

# RETURNING TO FIRST NATURE

## SEPARATION UNTO STARS AND SAND

The more separated into stars and sand I became the more different from others with painful disjunctures.

I was hateful cuz I didn't want them around, cuz I wanted them to PLEASE leave! It was social psychology.

I was on the extreme end of the bellshaped curve now and it was a rocky road until I totally relied on GOD.

The prickly females in town would come around to knock me off my perch. They were sooo treacherous.

My cat hisses when my dog busts her boundaries. Even if it's just a micrometer beyond point, that's it.

The saints have a stinging conscience. They're the ones grey with remorse, the others couldn't care less.

The narc's various moods are rapidly changing, inconsistent, fragmented and disconnected.

## TRAUMA BONDS SCREAM FOR CORRECTION

It's not that your missing that person but a wound inside that they have opened. Jenna Ryan

Overdependency on external source indicates core dependency needs undeveloped as a child.

You're longing for your self to meet those deep needs--the self given away to this person who's apathetic.

When you run after someone who is rejecting you're abandoning yourself, like you're not enough.

STOP the longing, START the rerouting. You deserve real love not this trigger for a festering inner wound.

You must be a bore if you have no haters whatsoever.

# RETURNING TO FIRST NATURE

Now's the time to dial it down about this guy. Once you see it triggered an early trauma, defy it.

Attractions: He triggered a trauma screaming for correction, that's all you gotta know about him.

The experience of the concentration camp left us in fear, apprehension and mental breakdown. Survivor

Things worked out instantly when I shifted focus from external validation to miracles of God within.

## LURKING FOR OLD FLAMES:  STOP IT

Seeking external validation shows incomplete development and these days we use the computer to do it.

After getting the headlines use the computer for movies or music. Switch validation back to God, feel it.

Once hurt like that I came solidly to the wheel at last and now NO one interrupts my flow and it's a blast.

I see so many emotionally fragmented women spending most of their days virtually lurking for old flames.

Virtual spying is a waste of time since they've evolved to new lives and are no longer the same, no jive.

## INDIVIDUATION FROM THE FAMILY SYSTEM

Individuation from the family mass is no easy task. It can be a violent juncture finding your Self at last.

The family is like peas in a pod and then there's you, the black sheep who loves God but is seen as odd.

They're all alike and then there's you, the free thinker seen as a terrible troublemaker and bad influence too.

# RETURNING TO FIRST NATURE

They fear your hypnotic influence as your eyes are bright, awake, profound, deep and they are dunces.

Schizophrenia is characterized by fusion to the family system, no differentiation = a psychic nothing.

Mom wanted to encourage my innate creativity but forced her illogical views on me which made me silly.

I knew they were ALL talking about me ALL the time but couldn't say it or be labeled paranoid psychotic.

Anyone seeing truth was labeled sick, mad or bad--a hater of family and to blame for everything, they said.

Their conversation was stuck on dull and small and anyone moving beyond that--REAL--was weird, that's all.

At a young age I felt the only answer was to get drunk and mimic the system exactly, personal dreams sunk.

## INSTINCTUAL KNOWLEDGE OF SYSTEMS

In grad school I had a flare/instinct for Systems Theory, being so familiar with the complex circuitry.

One serial family bully was the feminist sister who was so narrow she made them adapt to her completely.

The dysfunctional family is filled with secret coalitions and jealous, catty triangulations against the "One".

It's when the two older sisters have ONE raison d'etre: to GET HER and keep her down for good I'll betcha.

The "One" may be fragmented with trauma bonds and FUSED with this system that hates her/his guts.

Is there anything worse? I don't think so, fused to those gossiping old crones, life is nothing but low blows.

# RETURNING TO FIRST NATURE

We start with **ONE** creative member. The others hate him, in fear he develops a crutch and becomes a sinner.

Life is wonderful if adapted to brethren but if out of sync life grates instead and angry confusion sets in.

I didn't trust my sisters for their liberal views nor did they me since I was a conservative since age 12.

But they had the **POWER** being older and that dyad came against this little lass and it **STUCK** like that.

Sometimes the old guard has to literally die out before you can rise up. Just wait, your time will come luv.

I sensed the secret coalitions constantly and wanted only to flee. I was a lucky refugee, I got married.

My husband saw the sick Cinderella System and my prince wrenched me away for good to freedom.

## THEY'RE LIKE POOH ON THE SHOE

Like pooh on the shoe it keeps coming back so why we need a desktop Manual to keep us on track.

You're at the top of your game and it's outstanding, electric, cosmic, the apex--cuz you gotta fence.

Be yourself, incredible as usual. Style, magnetism, nerve, wit, grace and boldly/bluntly unstoppable.

Style is nothing you can fake--you're born with it. You either have it/not and when pretended it's rot.

I wanna build this airplane not get dragged into neighborhood politics and that's what's cosmic.

If you've a right to be mad, then squelching it will only bring stress, mental illness, disease/bad.

# RETURNING TO FIRST NATURE

If you don't even have a sense of order you're clearly of the devil joker.

He was a hick from the beginning & you thought you could change him.  Don't worry over enemies when you see em again old age got em.

Accept all delays as the fastest route.

I told you not to work, you did anyway so God took your computer away. Music hypnotizes pets so I can work.

Party for three days, blow it out. Think of green pastures, mellow out.

Anti-depressants for just two weeks caused mental illness for thirty years-- rages, divorces, tears.

How could it be that someone so entirely brilliant could get so messed up--the worst of the lot?

I hope you enjoy this journey through my mind. If you don't, kindly drop me and I'll attract my own kind.

If you think all those selfies are interesting you've got another thing comin'. Do something not just shovin'

**WORK ALL THE TIME/SELF-DETERMINED**

A genius is simply someone who works constantly but to keep it up takes his LEISURE seriously.

When I wanna work doesn't conform to time or place so that means no social for the ace.

Don't let anything--not one thing--track your mind. Now let it all come up from deep inside.

When God wants your own thing all else is static but since you've been tracked, you're still on it.

Insist on your right to sit/do nothing but look out the window. Meditation is most important dumbo.

# RETURNING TO FIRST NATURE

Don't let em tell you how to do it. Do it your way though it makes no sense, just the way you intuit.

You gotta catch crap when it happens. Nail it, something's wrong, use instinct hon'

Your project like the Taj Mahal: Attention to detail, incredible intricacy and beauty, intense focus.

The rest of the world is really creepy. Even the Europeans are liberals, letting em all in/a tragedy.

Because I relaxed, by refusing to work, I got the insight that collapsed the whole mess into a lark.

We had it so good, we were different in a rare experiment that worked until conquered by swine.

Think I'll refuse to work another day, it's so profitable and enriching, ok?

We had it so good, our men were decent. But we were debased into immorality four decades recent.

The barometer of barbarians is how they treat dogs and that's most of the world: want Americana!

## MOST OF THE WORLD IS REALLY CREEPY

Most of the world is really creepy but we were different.

Now the SJW starts up about how terrible America is.

Self-selling women really turn me off. Let it stand on it's own boss.

If you use your art to virtue signal on trendy topics you're not an artist. For art is eternal not this bull.

I don't virtue signal on trendy topics, I'm trying to undo all this.

Maslow said the superior man has only a few friends his whole life, so get a life.

# RETURNING TO FIRST NATURE

First they're your friend then compete with you in front of others--sign to drop em (false brothers).

If something doesn't add up, if it's stuck in your craw, if you can't get over it: bring it up, look at it.

If you sense exclusion or triangulation (two against one) see it as important and let it be central, hon'

Don't let things go by, you'll only stuff or smoke it down. Face it, discuss it, keep the day flowin'

The contagion of madness is such that we've made each other sick. Work on mixed signals, think.

Victimized, she became mentally ill in that system. Stockholm Syndrome: she took *donations* for him.

Their hate is a sign God's getting ready to bless you. So don't justify or explain, just bid them adieu.

Just by being yourself you unify all opposites. Refuse all categories and live your separate life.

Assembly of the wicked enclosed me, wild dogs surround me, a gang of evil men crowd around me.

They always hate you to begin with and can't wait to stab you in the back as soon as possible. True?

**PUT PAST IN A BAG, THROW IT OUT**

Put that whole bad era in a bag/throw it out.

Greatest suffering = greatest poetry. Relaxation = greatest creativity.

Just be in the groove: be a supple paint brush in God's hand, I behoove.

Relax and let God and the angels take the reins now. You've done the work so now recede, go low.

# RETURNING TO FIRST NATURE

You've checked to make sure it's all right. Now send it so all doors can open with God's might.

You were just the vessel for the Creative Act. Now that you've given birth, enjoy the fruits/just relax.

Having birthed the Creative Act you're also mature, it's the same path.

Insofar as you come to God you come to the True Self. For those talents were designed before birth.

If you've checked it, just send it. Now party until the benefits.

You plant a seed, you WAIT, you reap the harvest. It's not immediate--the waiting part is a must.

You did it. You went against the grain, you went with your instincts, you fought for privacy to do it.

It's not yours anymore, it belongs to the world. You were just the vessel for this magnificent work/wonder.

People of principal do what they say they will do and never lie. Compare that to today and cry.

You've done your work now you can be a child again. Just like Jesus said and it's the right brain.

## GENIUS KNOWS THE VALUE OF LEISURE

Take a day just for music, no left brain linearity. Now you'll feel an absolute torrent of creativity.

I'm done now I can just have fun.

There's a spirit of strife. She's cold to me but she's your friend so what is going on, I don't like.

It's all erased: that's the miracle of Jesus.

# RETURNING TO FIRST NATURE

Dear Lord please cleanse my memory. That's all we have and it can ruin one's whole life, believe me.

If you can't afford a house with a fence, rent a cabin in the wilderness. Solitude, escape the mess.

I was hurt not by him but the Wife of the Alcoholic Syndrome--after first drink anything can happen.

Women debased, hated/baited, called ugly/berated, scapegoated: became queens or didn't make it.

Reliance on God's grace relieves us of the burden to make it on our own: Through Him our star is shone.

Banish idols. Like how you sought approval of your sister/brother all your life-- love Jesus with out rival.

**JESUS SAID:  NO ONE'S GOOD!**

Jesus said "Don't call me good--only God is good." We're nothing but filthy rags with  a heart of wood.

Get honor, get affirmation, get recognition--and you'll be free? No it comes from Thee.

Conservatives: Watch what is put in your drink [to get dirt] by sex operatives.

If you want their approval you're gonna be waiting a long time. Give up on this, friends of mine.

Grace means: You don't have to do works/go to church. It is finished--Jesus died for the worst.

God had a perfect plan before my birth but I had to repent to find that groove, can you understand?

Not a bunch of books quickly finished but One good book that took a lifetime and becomes vintage.

They did the best they knew how, leave it at that.

# RETURNING TO FIRST NATURE

## WITHOUT GOSPEL IT'S ALL BABBLE

Without the true gospel they talk babble and lose the battle cuz it's God who wins over those who tattled.

There's only one way to get through to them—less words. That means increased boldness, it comes first.

Eloquence is a painting of the thoughts. - Blaise Pascal.

I'm in a peculiar position to write of the psychological conflict since I can still feel it/can't forget it.

The human genotype potential is true genius and you get it from overcoming obstruction: I want this.

Watch out for masks and never judge by appearances. Recall Lucifer is pretty with intelligences.

Things change, people age and die but still the baggage persists though God overcame the lie.

Stop obsessing over old hostilities. They're just actors used by God to punish/curb/heal, not enemies.

The answer to bad memories is to realize Jesus erases them--to the bottom of the sea (just don't go fishin').

## SINS ERASED FROM EAST TO WEST

As far as east is from west, that's how gone your sins are and now if you can forget you'll be a star.

No matter what you did for how long: with Jesus you're forgiven, it's forgotten, sins erased and it's done.

Sins are literally erased and that is the miracle of Jesus Christ--the good news after being disgraced.

# RETURNING TO FIRST NATURE

Sins erased, new life replaced, everything's forgiven but there's one problem: can you forget em?

That wasn't life trauma that was God breaking you down. It's part of the trip: potter's wheel, then renowned.

Passage of time and everything changes. But some hang on with lucid recall of events like the aged.

It's the story of the ages: You went so low but then up with the angels, a case of beauty from ashes.

Though salvation is free, like the saints my sins/remorse is ever before me but thankfully Jesus erases history.

I don't care if it's your family, this is as serious as it gets. No time for dogma freaks/brains in the pits.

Instead of including people, exclude. Jesus came to divide so get snippy/separate from all you despise.

Hypersensitives escape into sensual sins of self-indulgence to palliate shattered nerves/feeling rattled.

The great saints escaped into the desert wilderness first and came back after overcoming sin/the curse.

## SIN TO ESCAPE FATE BRINGS HATE

Though sin's an escape from fate it brings hate and that's the second obstacle building kings/the Great.

The saints went to the desert but came back: freshly endowed with all new powers, men of the hour.

Nature selects for adaptability not strength. Think of that when you lose it all and still it's God you thank.

Concupiscence: Man's tendency towards lust. It destroys his life as all he has turns to dust.

# RETURNING TO FIRST NATURE

If no one wants what you have so what--it's about your achieved reality, that's a fact.

People never seem to turn out as good as predicted. You get a glimpse of greatness then it's deflected.

Man is so evolved (to individualism) he has the capacity to delve into his interests in great depth.

But when man conforms--to his generations norms--he loses his unique genius and his work is corn.

Gotta make a dent while you're still here. Think of that always before it's too late and you disappear.

Just by you thinking back to pleasant times you reproduce it in your present situation as a hologram.

As soon as you find out who you are, you see God for who He is and it's a divine gift becoming His star.

If you don't hate evil as I do does that make you better than me, or worse? Tolerance is an evil word.

## BACK FROM THE BRINK, A PERFECT SAINT

When you suddenly re-appear so well they'll wonder if it ever happened (your journey through hell).

Gotta want something so bad you'll do anything for it. Like an artist loving beauty he comes alive to adore it.

My husband hates all that. He's a total white Christian conservative patriot/bigot and I love it.

Keep doin what you're doin', you are the best. God blesses humility as you approach the crest.

When the recovered blacksheep shaman returns to the tribe they stare and think "they must have lied".

# RETURNING TO FIRST NATURE

Just be happy you survived their system which warped you so bad it pulled you down, a twisted vixen.

With sin the cosmic egg breaks into a million pieces--from perfect order, synchronicity, joy and peace.

They get together and it's phonies and tongues wagging. A mutual admiration society of the dumbed/sagging.

When they're young and exposed to public fame it's good to describe hypocrisy to dull these flames.

Be foremost an intellectual and moral face of your time, a romantic soul hearing God's words sublime.

Poet not priest rules mankind. He explains past, dignifies present and predicts future (sees signs).

By deleting the world scene you'll be so much better. Happier, get your life back, more hours and power.

Decency of people shows in how they treat animals. Americans were decent but now we have criminals.

Perhaps you haven't been through enough devastation to realize the value of privacy but I have, it was dreary.

Stop thinking about everything you went through and just be grateful you got through it and no longer blue.

## EARLY GENIUS DEGRADES THE SAME

Early signs of genius then start getting lines, wrinkles, bloated areas, fuddy duddy, nothing extraordinary.

Most are so immature they can't stay steady. They vacillate from the right to the left: arrogant and heady.

It's the lure of sin that defies genius: They get out on a tangent as feet run to evil and it's the end of Eden.

# RETURNING TO FIRST NATURE

Concupiscence: man's tendency to lust. This takes the focus away from his work, turning to dust.

Concupiscence can be just as must for food as sex. It's anything that draws you from destiny: a hex.

I think it's arrogance/inhumility, sensual lust or prideful planning against foes that creates the tragedy.

By far the biggest detractor from genius is the need for social approval. This needs immediate removal!

Accepting sin will make you just as ugly as sin itself. It's about a beautiful spirit so against sin SHOW it.

Insofar as we come to God we come to the True Self He designed and that's your highest mind.

It can be done. Just keep doing what you do best and the pot of gold is eventually won (what fun).

Can he rise to the occasion, can he do his destiny, can he use the champion device of restriction?

## DESTINY DERAILED BY SENSUAL APPETITES

Is it destiny or derailed into sensual appetites? You can't have both: talents released when right.

These days anything goes and it's really (insanely) weird as human appetites fall to new lows.

Because of man's tendency to mis-apply intelligence, he must focus while using restrictiveness.

The social world is intelligence mis-applied. You're missing your real life sinning and it's all justified.

You'll have total relief after a lifetime of ceaseless and unappreciated work with so much grief!

# RETURNING TO FIRST NATURE

I pray you are hereby released from all phony, cold or treacherous attachments: cease!

Impatience is a problem and if you continue to force the fit you'll make a fool of yourself/be seen as illigit.

When the time comes to shine your light you'll be energized and catalyzed by God--it's outa sight!

You've been criticizing/seeing how they're wrong for years. Now just show the new way, free of tears.

You don't really know what the situation is between you and another so stay silent and altogether.

The female writer is so expressive (emotions) she must learn to not express to get to success.

Think interactionally all the way, like "she lives vicariously through her husband and it makes her snotty".

Put forth your various realities about the world of poverty ideation, sin, misery, disease and addiction!

Don't let the mundane world ever get you down. Refuse to answer but force them up, the clowns!

## DIVINE MIRACLES FROM LIVING RIGHT

I've experienced many divine miracles, all from living right and it's black and white from when I was pitiful.

There's a thing about nature when your heart is good: People take your hand and everything is understood.

You are not the person they say you are. Not a misguided/mischievous child but a budding star!

The more humble you are the more "it" will happen so handle this like a crate of eggs and don't be nappin'.

# RETURNING TO FIRST NATURE

They don't see the importance of relocation for liberals think all areas are alike--yikes, take a hike.

He's an entitled brat who needs to have his face slapped. You don't need an arrogant creep and dirty rat!

She has every right to be confident, she's won the right to be unique (no more up a creek).

All those things he's done but he can't be neat and orderly which is all I care about cuz to me it's Godly.

It was all demons. It wasn't you and it happens to all mankind until repentance changes the tide.

It's moving from a grenade range to a peaceful island. That's reacting to danger with strategic relocation.

Don't rely on others if they can throw you out. It's just not smart cuz things change quickly, or not.

## LOQUACITY:  PEOPLE TALK TOO MUCH

People talk too much. It's nervous chatter, shut up. Stop virtue signaling, be more like Trump.

They actually see themselves as loving! What a joke, showing dark auras of hatred as we spoke.

You are not wise feeling nostalgic over the past. The bible says it--the present is where it's at.

I'm just borrowing these mountains, enjoyed by generations through eternity

Here for now, tomorrow forever gone. Out out brief candle. Shakespeare

Hankering over the past--you do not inquire wisely concerning this, always searching for old bliss.

One isn't an artist just cuz they say they are.

# RETURNING TO FIRST NATURE

Be all sweetness and light. Even if you hate something, have aristocratic reserve about it/do it right.

You get used to living in squalor and desensitize to horror so soon you expect nothing more.

Neatnick females living with slobby men and visa versa: a terrible plight mal-adapting to such curses.

Neatnick women mal-adapting to slobs ends in depression, addiction or being strangely odd.

Keep comparing em to God. That's all you can do to remain sane and even turn it to your gain.

Live in the magic moment. It's yours, it's now, God's here, everything will be all-ok, God hears.

It's a terrible thing when a man falls off her pedestal--a sudden switch then she's done with it all.

Trouble? Open Psalms on persecution of the soul by those who consort with like minds so cold.

## HIGH WALLS, LOCKED GATE:  GOOD FATE

High walls, locked gate. Keep fair-weather friends out cuz they get irate and change your fate.

Don't say anything. You talk too much.

Shut up, I'm thinking. Some are a mental hazard with all their blathering--pure static and stinking.

Never adapt to time schedules always watch recordings when you want to.

God's timing: There comes a moment when the preparatory past splits from the blast (success at last).

Interactional templates/archetypes appear, no matter how rich it's still fear

# RETURNING TO FIRST NATURE

A discovery ties loose ends together, resolves contradictions, settles doubts and throws the rest out.

Discoveries are characterized by brutal reversals in perception.

One never knows when he will be done until that moment he is done. Albert Einstein

The superior man is scientist, artist and religious. Not a Buddha or an Einstein but both plus a great artist.

He who puts his hand to the plow and looks back is not fit for the kingdom, so stay present to bring it all on.

That was back then--an earlier phase, a cursed time so stay in the now, amen.

Just because you love Jesus doesn't mean you won't pay the piper so repent and be all the wiser.

If I look at the masses, I will never act. If I look at the One, I will. MotherTeresa

Look it up yourself, I say nothing untrue. This is poli-psych poetry--and it won't always please you.

## REPENT FOR SELF-LOVE OR ELSE

The only way to self-love is repentance. Not loving yourself madly while being a liar, thief or ass.

Devil in disguise: Lucifer is beautiful and smart so Paul warned hypocrites not to judge by appearances but the heart.

Evil associations corrupt--you can't swim in those waters and not get give up.

Another way of sayin' resistance builds muscle: "When the going gets weird, the weird turn pro". Hunter S. Thompson

Imagine an evil monster with a beautiful face. Now do the same as you discern the whole human race.

# RETURNING TO FIRST NATURE

You can try to please someone so much you end up killing them--that's the pathological system.

God judges the heart. Be sweet to animals, He'll see it and give a good mark

Separate from the lower, I'll give you the higher. I'll raise one up while the other's stuck in the mire.

If you're different your sins will stand out more, so repent to seem normal to them, the perceivers.

Just say "help me" and He'll fill in the spaces. No need for longwinded prayers or church auspices.

God's discipline (punishments) can last decades so be cautious of your sin-sensual escapades.

God hates, gets angry and punishes: we love Him for this attribute of justice.

Their houses are gas chambers turgid with waves of chemicals. But only the sensitive can know this pal.

Why does it feel like heaven to flirt with hell? Cuz sin has a lure so ignore what you feel or go under it's spell.

The inferior man has no concept of order. He'll deliberately mess you up/frustrate your plans, for sure.

All of life is a game, haven't you heard? Play it, play it well and you will win by overcoming the herd.

**FRIENDSHIPS ARE TESTED AND TRIED!**

Friendships are tested in tough times. You can't come back now I'm rich oh frenemies of mine.

Things go well until they don't. Don't get complacent: plan well, drop your loser friends then the throne.

Walk into a house, it hits me like a wave--greyness where there was color, nausea/ dizziness when it was ok.

# RETURNING TO FIRST NATURE

It's relieving to know all those years of moral insanity were demons in reality.

The past is an anchor to things you can't change. God says move ahead and everything's arranged.

Holding onto the past is the same as being anchored to it. Forget it!

The devil wants you mired in the past like quicksand--stuck in it. God says no blessings unless rid of it.

Being stuck in the past is victim mentality and the devil's lies. Knowledge is power--escape his device!

The past is not yours, just the present and things to come. But look back and you lose all this fun.

False doctrine is a harlot and thus the Jezebel spirit seeks to strip away truth from those believing it.

Peace doesn't remove the storm, it gets you through it. Oh how we need more of the holy spirit! A. Rowe

Healing waters and miracle oils are abominations of witchcraft and spoil.

In having to return to the original system I lost all my identity and relapsed into hellish misrepresentation.

## GOD USES ENEMIES TO DISCIPLINE YOU!

God uses your enemies to discipline you. Then if you repent He turns it on them and He can be cruel!

They felt superior, they excluded you. You adapted by thinking that too, but now with inversion, whew!

You do good work, you oughta be recognized--justly remunerated too--so God took care of it, whew.

When you finally pop into fame and fortune, your day's are the same: just do what's in front of you, ok?

# RETURNING TO FIRST NATURE

If you're gonna lead the tribe you'd better have high morals--or get weak and be trampled by vandals.

Keep posting and give it time to digest. After all it's most important: it's about saving the West.

The Lord says to visit the widow. Why is that? Because it's the worst possible thing, ya know.

Please tell everyone I'm gonna write my own history so please don't remind me.

Be old, enjoy being old, for you'll never be old again. You'll get a new body in heaven, forever young and thin.

Cabin life showed me eternity and simplicity not the domestic comfort of homey extravagance/grandiosity.

Mental illness taught me how people treat the mentally ill but with repentance I'm so much smarter still.

I never wanted all those people around, I was just too weak to make them leave then they kept me down.

Your worst enemies were jokers swept up. The weak are swept up and away after they've had their day.

**FINDING THE QUINTESSENTIAL-ONLY**

Having found the quintessential in a cabin, when I expanded operations but didn't add = fabulous!

Much of mental illness is just moral madness from going against your and God's will, I remember it still.

Retirement is when you can just stay home. That's what you always wanted anyway, your throne.

Once you see the light God removes the thorn-in-your-side teaching it to you and now you're perfect, whew.

# RETURNING TO FIRST NATURE

As you look back put it all in the same bag: "Stuff I Went Through". Now throw the dam bag out--pooh.

Go from the presence of a foolish man, when thou perceivest not in him the lips of knowledge. Prov. 14:7

Too few rejoice at a friend's great fortune and the greatest human emotion is jealousy (just imagine).

The wicked forces bring darkness, poverty, pain and betrayal. They seek to steal, destroy and kill.

Be sober, be vigilant; because your adversary the devil, as a roaring lion walketh about seeking whom he may devour. 1 Peter 5:8

Always reduce things to their simplest terms, then you can see what's going on. Remove superfluity, you've won.

Arrogance precedes ruin unless you repent. Then you're a shoe-in as perfect and good as it gets.

To gain strength and wisdom the prophetess exiled to the desert wilderness: alone in a cabin for 31 years.

## IT WASN'T THEM, *SIN* BRINGS ATTACKS

It wasn't them, sin brings attacks. It's not people but dark forces evoked by our bad behavior/being asses.

No worries. You work and work and when the time comes God'll bring you forward--just nothing untoward!

Only the weak are cruel. Gentleness is only expected of the strong. Leo Buscaglia

You got it all cuz of what you went through and overcame. You're punished or rewarded--that's the game.

These crazy days it's important to simplify, constantly. That's the road to inner-amplify: bliss for free.

# RETURNING TO FIRST NATURE

Keep simplifying--so you're always cutting through the chaos, coming back to your matrix: this is selfix.

Watching old movies makes me happy. Like a time capsule I switch eras and the tension leaves instantly.

Light music to evoke thought, looking at the mountain views. That's the limit of chaos--to the news, pooh.

Get the headlines here, back to light music and mountain views, walks with dogs, beauty and gratitude!

Eldering is about purifying the moment to enable lucid recall of the details of previous moments:  gems.

Eldering is about savoring and that's only done by eliminating and decluttering and that's a big thing.

Sagacious eldering is about the temporal lobes exploding open to eternity: panoramic vision!

Whether stuck up or not, you don't wanna seem like you are. Go the other way: be a sweet and humble star.

## ARROGANCE PRECEDES RUIN

Arrogance precedes ruin and arrogant rulers fall. The only solution:  stay humble ya'll.

Mom was my best teacher even though she had to be drunk to confront. I'm sober but extremely blunt.

By interrupting me constantly she was a dominator. I could never think deep, kept in the backseat.

If they're not on board cut em off. It's come to that: remember the cruelty of those sho scoffed.

Avoid anything that tracks: That would be TV, news, movies, books, chats. Just music/nature is max.

# RETURNING TO FIRST NATURE

You can't hurt us. Your acts are so dishonorable you actually empower us sweetheart, the more you fuss.

I graduated from all that and am not going back. Try it buddy I'll reject you cuz you don't have my back.

Don't fret cuz the best draws critics but that provides the resistance to build the very best there is.

Never be discouraged by a creep. They're doing the devil's work by making you look cheap/black sheep.

They are ignorant, self-delusional and arrogant. The latest: if a man smiles at a woman he's sexist.

**MIXED SIGNALS OF THE RABBLE**

His words were respectful but the implication rude.

For I know the plans I have for you...to prosper and not harm you, to give you hope and a future. (Jeremiah 29:11)

Don't expect bad things cuz the past was worst of everything. It was just a lesson about wages of sin (like a fling).

I ran from the party escaping back to the house where it's just so or: acid, choking/waking up hoarse.

I won't say all is poison but just about. I'm staying home from now on, let him run around and go out.

I still say if they don't have the problem they're not gonna handle things the same way. Don't go there, ok?

If you have this problem you'll take additional steps. If you don't you just stay as you are and remain inept.

Yours is just a big smile like Obama--fake. You're not really happy/nice (I know) and you're on the take.

# RETURNING TO FIRST NATURE

To get to the top, let go of petty jealousies on the bottom then zoom up and you won't be forgotten.

Eldering is when you pass on the keys to the tribe. You've honed your talent, best in the field and nice.

The happy person has joy, optimism, creativity, warmth and adventure: it's from God and it's true allure.

You simply can't adapt to the herd and be your unique self. Be nice/sweet but stay the magic elf.

PTSD: You only feel the traumatic stress after the noxious event when you're in safety and can vent.

PTSD: The devil's crowd had such an effect you went crazy. It was a mal-adaptation to liberals maybe.

## DON'T SUCCUMB: RISE ABOVE PTSD

PTSD is when you can't get over it. You've escaped to paradise but still suffer as if you're in it. Rise above it.

Don't feel bad about feeling sad after escaping to paradise. That's PTSD: suffering after destruction/lies.

Elder mysticism resembles infantilization or psychosis. Is this the inner journey or PTSD after that awful crisis?

Inner Journey or PTSD? Stress is a natural reaction to the traumas we went through in the liberal half century.

Sometimes you can't see all the hell you went through till it's over. That's PTSD: suffer for eventual closure.

Keep hope of another world burning: of prosperity and innovation, of kids going moral and really learning.

The herd of hicks get miffed you don't think like them. A mature genius must cut em all lose, my friend.

# RETURNING TO FIRST NATURE

If one's motives are good he can be as arrogant and conceited as he pleases.

To be "nice" they spout crap and lie to not rock the boat. They avoid disapproval but it's cut-throat.

The mal-adaptation to hostile environments (characterized by mixed signals) is exhaustion.

They thought they were superior as part of the herd. Now deflated and powerless: theatre of the absurd.

The childhood of famous writers was sad. They transmuted this to good but many died of drink or other bad.

Divine vindication is necessary for the relief of the saints. God always gets the haters, since the ancients.

Enemies: Their time is comin'--you'll even feel sorry for em--so just keep truckin and let God handle em.

**FORGIVE BUT NOT FORGET**

Forgiving and forgetting are two separate things, unfortunately. My sins are ever before me, prophets say.

If you find your groove in cocky self-assertion God designed you that way to present truth to the morons.

Now's the time to get hep: weed your friendship garden and then you'll have success and God's pardon.

Most people are stupid. They weren't born that way it's deliberately planned and they're also polluted.

Isn't it interesting people behaving like fiends while always claiming to be about love, light and peace!

Know your friends from your enemies--cordial with "frenemies" but there's a wide gulf, believe me.

**GOD SAID THERE'S NO LUKEWARM**

# RETURNING TO FIRST NATURE

God said there's no lukewarm and it's the same with friends. Cordial to frenemies but that is the end.

You must know the foe. Only a weak neurotic goes into denial about this--it's your life, you know.

Your circle must empower you and think you're great cuz you are, not jealous of you cuz you're a star.

Some people are backstabbers and you know the signs. You felt it in your gut since junior high.

Bad associations are a sin and a block. They are described in Psalms: read them and be shocked.

The wicked are weak and can't help but mess you up, discredit, empty your cup or belittle nonstop.

The problem is obstruction and it's usually a person. Cut em loose, you've got plenty of reasons.

If they think they're better than you you gotta break it or they'll invade your day and make you pay.

## SELF-CHOSEN FAMILIES

The utter importance of family is a given but sometimes it must be self-chosen and I'm for that, amen.

They can probably love but it sure wasn't you. That's the point--move on and start something new.

Reject the faithless and a terrible burden is lifted. What a relief: full recovery after being emotionally jilted.

Cu em loose and never look back. They had their chance, time for your attention to deflect to the Elect.

Once you recognize the enemy you will feel so free! Just from putting him in the right (foe) category.

Gossip-called-"concern". They knew exactly what they were doing when against you the town turned.

# RETURNING TO FIRST NATURE

It's called calumny: they murdered your reputation and they're gonna have to pay for it, it's that serious.

Those who have adapted to dysfunction early can't read the fact that their associates are the enemy.

Growing up in environments where everybody lies, they flirt with danger later and can't see through disguise.

Those who will see who your mutual friends are in order to get them to drop you, block them too.

If there's something wrong you know it (in your gut the solar plexus) but may deny it to keep it: don't do it.

Loving Pollyanna get off your high horse.

They castigate you for not being more "loving" when they are so hateful, you can tell by their scoffing.

## SOCIAL IS NOT SUPERIOR

Since being "social" is a superior trait to them, they tolerate inferior relationships/fair-weather friends.

Bad associations maintain the sins used as a device to mal-adapt to them. See this and sin will end.

Drinking/drugging are mal-adaptive coping mechanisms. It's the way a genius may cope with dopes.

Say no (the most important word) and then turn: your attention to the fascinating and beautiful wider world.

Cut these obstructions loose and then be a strong survivor. Now don't look back but enjoy your revival.

People are cruel so be careful who you let in. If inconsistent always flip-flopping they're not your friend.

They criticize me for telling the truth and upsetting people. They would never do that so they lie and it's evil.

# RETURNING TO FIRST NATURE

To stave off aggression or get protection: is that why we make friends? If it is, life's been hellish, amen?

When I just started being myself friends came from all directions, no need to be friending for protection.

Make your preparations then escape into music. Stay sane in an insane world which is so crazy/tragic.

A strong mind learns the truth and remains unswerving. A weak mind sees the truth but changes, a dumb earthling.

A weak mind sees the truth then flips cuz he talked to someone else. Very dangerous, don't trust the louse.

Because you don't agree with them they say you have a mental illness. Cut em loose and return to stillness.

Sense rejection, reject them back. They don't have your back so get hep quick, no trust, rise above crap.

Depression RX: Medical cannibus would change and return you to the right brain/a colorful fascinating cornucopia.

## COMMUNISM TRIGGERED BY RACISM

Downfall: Lakes of muck, stinking garbage, shabby stores, cig hawkers and strange smells.

Don't we want to be more clever than our ancestors who let themselves be burned? Lodz ghetto

If I told you everything I know you could not sleep. This way, I alone cannot sleep. Ghetto Leader

Bad ideas quickly congeal into conventional wisdom then it's too late--nip em in the bud to stay first rate.

Definition: If they took orders from the Deep State this is called BETRAYAL and they will be executed.

# RETURNING TO FIRST NATURE

They didn't have to kill the baby--if they drank adrenochrome for vanity they're guilty: crimes against humanity.

A time is coming when men go mad attacking someone who isn't mad saying "you're mad--not like us".

It's communism under the guise of socialism, evoked by issue of "racism" but that's just the trigger son.

The new virulent secular religion of WOKE is what I've been fighting for decades [they attacked after I spoke].

Goal: to make you hate yourself, your country and the constitution--once its gone you're under UN control.

Parents of trannies: screwing em up, giving them attention for something that's not in their code.

Son/daughter is a tranny cuz he gets attention from liberal feminist mommy by acting crazy that way.

## HISTORICAL REVISIONISM

In the West we only punish the guilty, not their descendants, group or family.

Like all men our founders had flaws but the virtues they brought to our country make it the best place to be.

WHY this country is special/WHY it needs to be defended: by keeping monuments that explain it.

SAY IT: This is NOT about equality but a radical revision of our history and we won't stand for it!

In a war to free the slaves, a million white men lost their lives or legs--tell that to the dumbed down kids.

The more we focus on Founder's flaws the less we see the influence of VIRTUE and their dedication to God.

# RETURNING TO FIRST NATURE

The lessons from national monuments are what we want to teach our children--this is no small thing!

These were lessons learned as **KIDS** and now as adults we **SEE** this: the immoral desecration of monuments.

Statue desecration is the result of Christ taken out of America and also the trigger for **JUDGEMENT**.

As a kid I was so impressed with Mt. Rushmore and now they wanna add Obama--the great destroyer?

Our statues stand for principals imbedded in our minds so to see them desecrated is literally sickening.

Wow: Listen to me folks, they're doubling down on their hoax. Use Vitamin C, D and zinc not masks.

The virus incubates in cloth whereas without masks it would just disperse--take C, D and zinc first.

The party should be outlawed and made illegal. It's never been sicker or more destructive.

Never surrender to the Culture Jihadists who demand you let them destroy your history!

## HIX PEEVED OVER POLITIX

Peeved over politics. People are dividing and it's all political--they're getting violent and hypocritical.

What will happen in the next 50 days: will our new year be glorious with hope or ablaze?

You got into trouble cuz everything you did you did in a big way. It was just the wrong direction, ok?

They're all about how nice they are but I sense pit vipers! I will trust my instincts are stay away, for sure.

# RETURNING TO FIRST NATURE

She doesn't have empathy to understand lack of immunity. You're not sick just sensitive and that she can't knowith see.

We were thrown together, non-birds of a feather. It was miserable weather defending our identity, whatever.

It's important to know the foe but most are in denial about their closest friends and family: frenemies.

Every tongue that rises up against you shall fail. Let the herd of hicks blab all they want it'll be to no avail.

85% of communication is non-verbal, so don't listen to words--read body language signs if you're able.

Life is about stages and this is the highest stage, understand? It is most grand and that's the apex, man.

Don't let the grandkids over if immoral/sinful with cultural demons. That's your job, to teach em.

## THE MORE LOFTY THE HIGHER THE WALLS

The higher in station the more necessity for walls. So why you letting em in/they don't have to call?

You've worked all your life to get to this point. You're not about to mess things up, so God will anoint.

Men can't help a woman get ahead, lacking a theoretical foundation they have to steal it all instead.

Don't give em a chance to come to the door. Keep gate locked and announce before seeing the star.

No more dropping by. You live a formal life now, not mal-adapting to interruptions and invasions.

When scared look up, look up, look up.

Your job is to educate the heart.

# RETURNING TO FIRST NATURE

False friendly: you are "family" until you don't fit then you're out: the system blocks creative spout.

You can't stand contradiction so you analyze it to death. They don't care to--they can live with the mess.

You can't stand contradiction--an inconvenient person--so you're edged into outlaw status: vermin.

You're smart, they're not. You don't fit, they can live in this tangled knot.

It's not bitchiness it's acerbic punditry.

Genius makes it big if he endures being slurred without taking a swig before his gig so just persevere, ya dig?

You can't accept things that don't make sense while they could care less: why genius dies early I guess.

You're "family" until you don't buy it then they ostracize: The human system cuts you down to size.

"At that time I will reverse your captivity and restore your fortunes". It's about timing, understand?

I love God cuz He understands when no one else does. He made me this way: different just because.

## MAGIC OF STARVATION

I don't like it when fasting groups become competitive. It's an inner journey man, none of anyone's business.

Avocado makes the fruit diet do-able.

"Humans live on 1/4 of what they eat. On the other 3/4 lives their doctor". Egyptian Pyramid Inscription

A little starvation can do more than the greatest doctors or medicines. Mark Twain

# RETURNING TO FIRST NATURE

Fasting evokes the sirtuin proteins which are responsible for DNA repair, the key factor in longevity.

Why would one eat if they are not hungry? It's most important to NOT EAT, not to eat.

Fasting promotes the growth of new neurons in the brain, a protection from Parkinson's and Alzheimers.

With Intermittent Fasting you have 16 hours a day to grow new brain neurons, meaning brilliant creations.

Optimal Neuronal Functioning is the result of eating less or fasting. Feel this in your coordination/bending.

An Extended Fast [EF] can reset your eating preferences. That's why we go longer, it reduces cravings.

Even fasting groups on Facebook will say "eat something" when you feel bad--I can't understand that.

When you finally come out [After your EF, your Trump card] you'll be a tidal wave, finally discovered.

You get to the point where even the right foods make you sick. Time for EF [extended fast]: God's little trick.

This is the thing about eldering or old age: As the body recedes, the brain expands [see em that way].

## RECAP THOUGHTS

Contrary to liberalism disparate outcomes doesn't show racism but demoralization/family breakdown.

You'll be constantly getting new ideas but the trick is how do you store them? Become an organizational genius.

If you're introverted you don't want any attention. It's something to get used to if in a profession.

## 100 KAREN KELLOCK BOOKS

AFFINITY OR MISERY
AGELESS CORNUCOPIA
AMERICA AWAKE!
AMERICA'S DAFT ERA
ARTS OF PALEO FASTING
AUTOPHAGY ON CHEATERS
BACKSTABBING NEUROTICS
BETRAYAL TRAUMA
BOOMERS AND BROKENNESS
BOOT ON NECK
CHAMPION GUIDES
COMMIE NUTHOUSE
COMMIES
COMMUNIST SPIRIT
CONTAGION OF MADNESS
CONTAGIOUS MADNESS
CULTURE CLASH BASHED
DAFT LEFT
DAILY FASTARIAN
DAM RATS
DIVERSITY IS CRUELTY
E-RACE WHITE
EVIL FREAKS (Beyond Gross)
THE END OR A BEND?
FEMALE BULLIES AND FEMI-NAZIS
FEMALE CARNALITY
FEMALE DUMB DOWN
FEMALE POWER DRIVE
FEMINISM AND RUIN 1 & 2
FIX FOR MISFITS
FOOLS & TRAMPS
FREEDOM SPEAKING
FRENEMY ENABLER
FRENEMY LIAR
FRENEMY THIEF
FRENEMY TRAITOR
TRENEMY TYRANT
GENIUS IS HELD DOWN
GLOBALISLAM
GOD USES THE FLAWED
HAZE OF THE LATTER DAYS

THE HERD IN WORDS
HIX POLITIX
HOW THEY RUINED US
JUST SKIP DINNER
LE FEMME AND THE COMMUNIST SPIRIT
LIBERAL CHAOS & ROT
LIBERAL DOUBLETHINK
LIBERAL GALL 1 & 2
LIBERAL SHOVE-DOWNS
LOCK YOUR GATE
LOSERS and Femme Fatales
MANUAL FOR SUPERIOR MEN
MODERN ART FROM HELL
MOSTLY FAKE
NOTES TO CHAMPS 1 & 2
OVERCOME FRENEMIES
PC MAKES US CRAZY
PEOPLE ARE CRUEL
PEOPLE PROBLEMS 1 & 2
PERSECUTED GENIUIS
POLI-PSYCH MYSTERIES
PRETENTIOUS SLOBS
QUEEN BEE
RED NEW DEAL
RETURNING TO FIRST NATURE
SEASON OF TREASON
SEPARATE MEANS HOLY
SOCIAL HYPNOTISM
SOLITUDE SOLUTION
SUPERCILIOUS
THE SCHOOLS SCREWED EM UP
TOAD TO PRINCE
TRIALS CYCLES
TRUMP VS. GROUP
TRUST IN TRASH
THE TRUTH ABOUT PEOPLE
UNDERHEANDEDLY CLEVER
WALK TALL WITHIN WALLS
WE'RE NOT ALL ONE
WINNERS SKIP DINNER
WORK OR SMERK

# KAREN KELLOCK PH.D.

M.S. Political Science, San Diego State.  Ph.D. in Psychology, University of California Irvine.  Postdoctoral:  UCI School of Medicine, Dept. of Psychiatry [NIMH Grants].  Developed the Debris Theory of Disease, a theory of system pathology in 120 books and 22 textbooks for the general public.  The theory has a general formula:  All disease is obstruction, all recovery is elimination, all success is attraction.  The three obstructions are people, habit and food. Remove obstruction and snap to your goals, waiting in the wings.